SPAIN

WORLD ADVENTURES

BY STEFFI CAVELL-CLARKE

BookLife

Written by:
Steffi Cavell-Clarke

Designed by:
Natalie Carr

A catalogue record for this book
is available from the British Library.

SPAIN
WORLD ADVENTURES

CONTENTS

Words in **bold** can be found in the glossary on page 24.

WHERE IS SPAIN?

Spain

Spain is a country in southwest Europe. The capital city of Spain is called Madrid.

SPAIN

4

Barcelona

The **population** of Spain is over forty-six million. Most people in Spain live in the big cities, such as Madrid and Barcelona.

WEATHER AND LANDSCAPE

Spain has a fairly warm climate. In the summer, Spain is usually very warm and sunny.

Spain has long stretches of beach and high mountains. Lots of **tourists** visit Spain for the sunny weather and to spend time on the beaches.

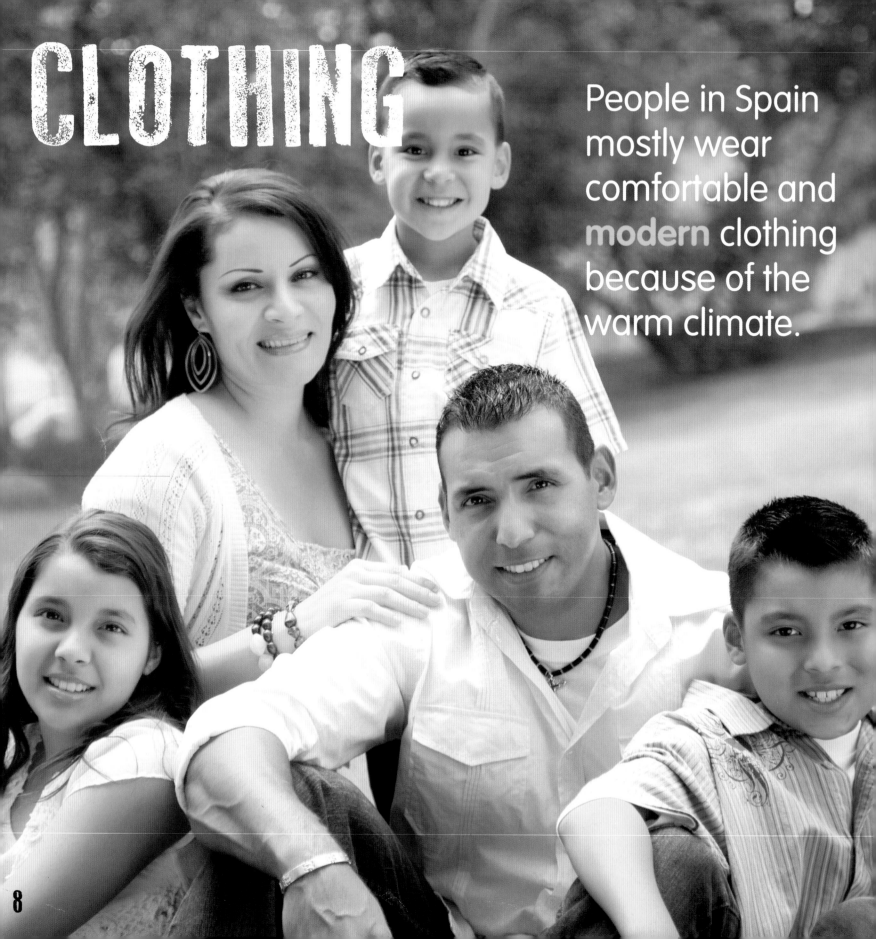

CLOTHING

People in Spain mostly wear comfortable and **modern** clothing because of the warm climate.

At **festivals**, Spanish people often wear **traditional** clothing. Female dancers wear long dresses in bright colours.

Flamenco Dancer

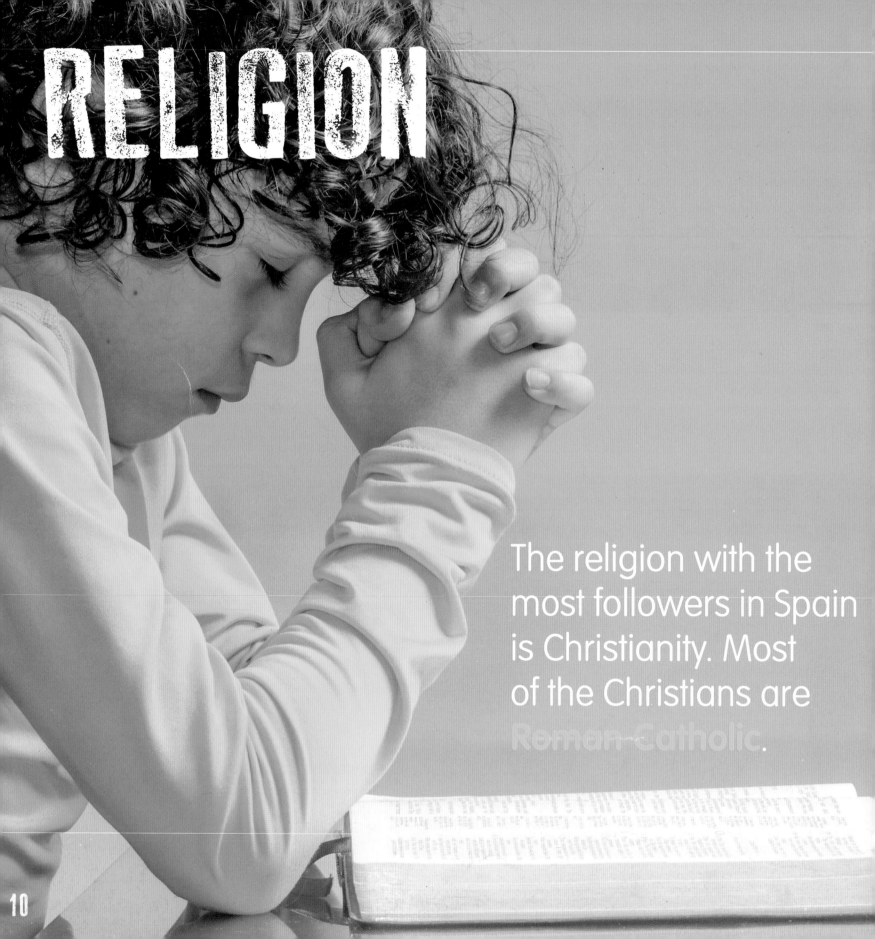

RELIGION

The religion with the most followers in Spain is Christianity. Most of the Christians are Roman Catholic.

The Roman Catholic place of **worship** is a church.
They visit the church every Sunday for prayer.

Sagrada Familia

FOOD

Paella

One of the traditional meals in Spain is called Paella. It is a spicy rice dish, which can have meat, fish and vegetables in it.

Tapas is also very popular in Spain. Tapas is a group of small bowls of tasty food, such as olives and seafood and special breads.

Olives, Fresh Seafood

AT SCHOOL

Children in Spain start school at the age of six. They study lots of subjects, such as Spanish, science, geography and maths.

Some children also go to after-school clubs, where they can play games and sports. Lots of children love to play football.

AT HOME

In towns and cities, many people in Spain live in modern flats.

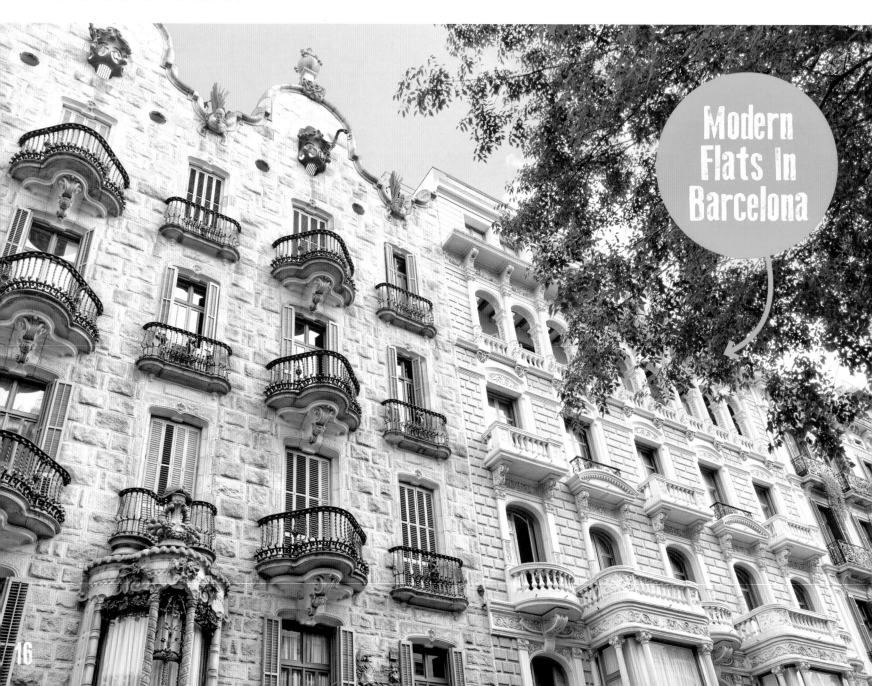

Modern Flats In Barcelona

There are also lots of farms in Spain. Farmers grow lots of crops, such as oranges, lemons and olives.

Most children live with their parents and siblings. Parents tend to go to work while the children go to school.

Spanish families like to get together for special occasions, such as weddings and religious holidays.

Real Madrid
Football Team

Football is the most popular sport in Spain. The top football clubs in the country are Real Madrid and FC Barcelona.

Other sports, such as tennis and basketball, are also very popular in Spain.

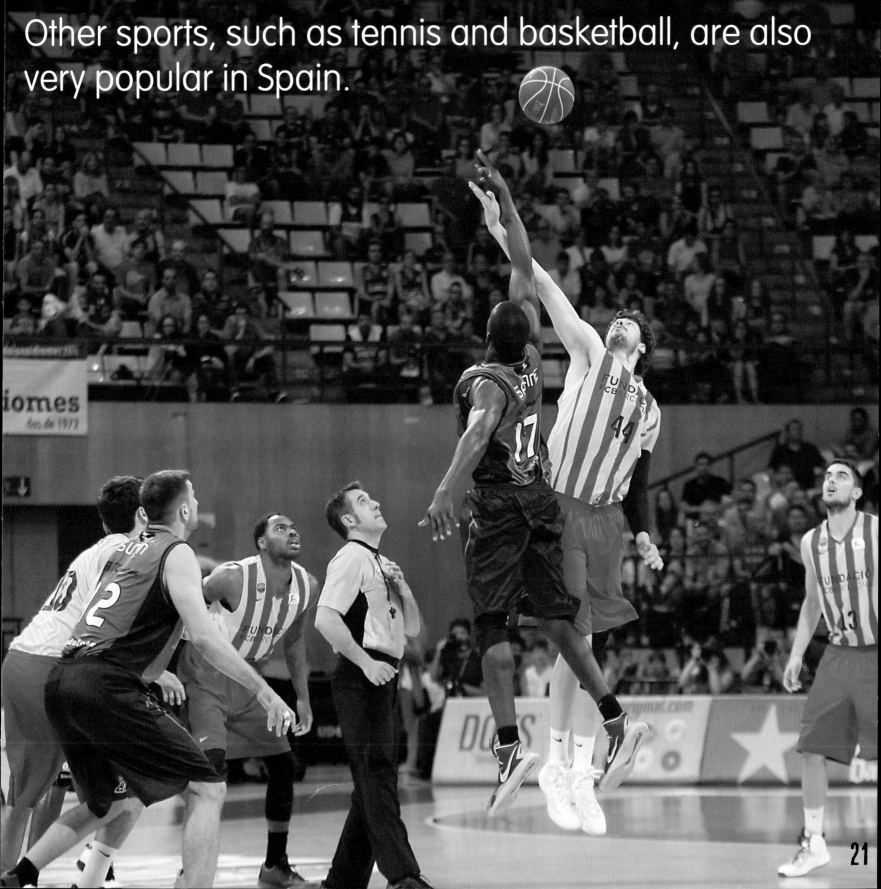

FUN FACTS

Spain has its own royal family. They live in a large palace outside the city of Madrid.

Royal Palace Of Madrid

The Flamenco is a Spanish dance. People dance the Flamenco on special occasions.

GLOSSARY

climate: the weather in a large area

festivals: special occasions that are celebrated

modern: something that has been made using recent ideas

population: amount of people living in that place

Roman Catholic: a type of Christianity

siblings: brothers and sisters

tourists: visitors from other country

traditional: ways of behaving that have been done for a long time

worship: a religious act such as praying

INDEX

Photocredits: Abbreviations: l-left, r-right, b-bottom, t-top, c-centre, m-middle.
All images are courtesy of Shutterstock.com.

Front Cover – Aleksey Klints. 2 – Luciano Mortula. 3 – Juriah Mosin. 4bl – Artgraphixel. 5 – Kanuman. 6 – Valeri Potapova. 7 – Djinn. 8 – Andy Dean Photography. 9 – nikitabuida. 10 – rmnoa357. 11 – Marina99. 12 – Iryna Denysova. 13 – Igor Dutina. 14 – Oksana Kuzmina. 15 – 2xSamara.com. 16 – Brian Kinney. 17 – bikeriderlondon. 18 – Monkey Business Images. 19 – Monkey Business Images. 20 – Natursports. 21 – Natursports. 22 – S-F. 23 – SandiMako. 24 –